KEN SMITH

LANDSCAPE ARCHITECT

Introduction by John Beardsley

The Monacelli Press

CONTENTS

Introduction: Lines of Work

John Beardsley

Dig into the projects presented in this book—which effectively constitutes a midcareer retrospective of Ken Smith's work—and you may find yourself wondering: What on earth does he think he is up to? Is he a landscape architect or an installation artist? A public servant or a provocateur? An elite gardener or a populist? A careful site sculptor or an in-your-face simulator? The perplexing truth is that Ken Smith is unapologetically all of these things—and others as well. In the space of two short decades, he has worked on an astonishing array of projects, from public parks in Toronto, Santa Fe, and Orange County, California, to private gardens in posh communities like Sagaponack, New York; from over-the-top art installations of glowing topiary, artificial stone, and plastic flowers to serene urban plazas in Manhattan, a colorful public schoolyard in Queens, and a community garden in Brooklyn. All of which prompts yet another question: How on earth are we to make sense of this?

It might help to know that Smith regards his practice as in some ways analogous to a fashion house, with different product lines for different market niches. Just as a clothing designer might produce both haute couture and prêt-à-porter, Smith responds to various client demands, from private to public, from high-end to pro bono. He also likens his training to that of a budding fashion designer, someone who works in another shop—in his case, the various offices of Peter Walker and Martha Schwartz—before taking a distinctive silhouette and starting his own house. While analogies between fashion and landscape architecture might seem a stretch, Smith is quick to point to the efforts of curators and writers like Richard Martin and Harold Koda to present fashion as a sophisticated art with its own cultural histories, whether in the service of elite or popular culture. Their attention to their subject as social phenomenon as well as medium and craft suggests that an equally careful interrogation of the modes, meanings, and cultural uses of landscape is possible—which is very much what Ken Smith is about. Whatever the intended audience for his work and however much humor or provocation it might express, Smith wants to be sure you know he takes his work seriously—and he wants you to take it seriously too.

It might also help to know that Smith came of age as a designer in the late 1980s and early 1990s, when the discourses of art were dominated by questions of representation, especially ideas around the appropriation and redeployment of found objects along with imagery and materials from mass culture. Smith was no stranger to these questions: as a precocious kid growing up in Iowa in the 1960s and 1970s, he was a regular visitor to the Des Moines Art Center, then amassing a significant collection of pop art by figures including Andy Warhol, Robert Rauschenberg, and Jasper Johns. His interest in representation was later honed by reading the work of the French cultural critic Jean Baudrillard, whose essays in the book *Simulacra and Simulation* suggested that an attachment to the "real" was being replaced by an affection for the copy, and that simulations in any event were being supplanted by wholly invented environments—simulacra—for which no precedent exists in the real world: think Disney, where space and time are collapsed into landscapes that bear little relation to history or geography as once we thought we knew them.

Smith's engagement with appropriation and simulation was reinforced in his earliest work with Martha Schwartz. He joined the Office of Peter Walker and Martha Schwartz in time to do "some lowly production work" on Schwartz's Splice Garden for the roof of the Whitehead Research Institute in Cambridge, Massachusetts (1986). The garden featured two zones of plastic shrubs and Astroturf, one suggestive of a Japanese garden, the other of formal French parterres; the two zones were "spliced" together to evoke the genetic research pursued at the institute. Appropriation and simulation continue to be central to Smith's work, particularly in his use of gaudy artificial flowers for the Hotel Eden and Cooper-Hewitt Triennial WallFlowers installations, or fake rocks and plastic boxwoods for his rooftop "camouflage garden" for the Museum of Modern Art in 2005. Smith's strategies confirm his engagement with the notion that nature in our time is entirely constructed: even climate, as Bill McKibben argues in his depressing book *The End of Nature*, is a product of culture.

The young designer also became attentive to explorations of seriality and repetition, for instance in the sculpture of minimalist artists such as Carl Andre and Donald Judd. Smith's subsequent use of these devices, however, might owe more to the music of composers like John Cage, Steve Reich, or John Zorn than to sculpture: while minimalist sculpture might be broadly and crudely characterized as sticking with patterns,

contemporaneous music was more apt to toy with them through delays, slippages, or overlaps, harnessing improvisation through flexible compositional formats. Several of Smith's current projects reveal an abiding interest in shifting systems of order over space. The Cooper-Hewitt Triennial WallFlowers and the Orange County Preview Park both present organized systems altered by random selection. At the Cooper-Hewitt, the locations of large and small flowers were determined by drawing numbers out of a bowl; at Orange County, elements were selectively removed by drawing lots.

Smith's interest in seriality was confirmed by his early work with Peter Walker, just as his affection for off-the-shelf materials and pop imagery was nurtured by his work with Martha Schwartz. He joined their joint practice in New York in 1986; when that office closed in 1988, he migrated to their office on the West Coast. He describes "a wild time out there" when they were all under one roof. He was the only designer working exclusively with Schwartz in the more experimental wing of the practice, in what he recalls "was derisively termed

John Beardsley

the playpen." When the Office of Peter Walker and Martha Schwartz dissolved in 1990, Schwartz, Smith, and David Meyer joined forces to create a new firm. Smith's principal project was the one-acre Village of Yorkville Park in Toronto, the result of a competition for which he was the lead designer. Although the firm dissolved in 1992, Smith would continue to work with Meyer on the Yorkville project through its completion in 1994.

Meanwhile, Smith moved back to New York in July 1992, where he established his own firm, if fitfully at first. "I wanted to return to New York. But I came back without prospects or work." He taught at the City College of New York, the Universities of Pennsylvania and Virginia, and the Harvard Graduate School of Design; at the same time, he participated in exhibitions and entered competitions. The Glowing Topiary Garden for Liberty Plaza in New York, with lighting designer Jim Conti, in the winter of 1997 was, Smith recalls, "the first project people took notice of." A seasonal installation of 16-foot-tall cones lit from within by colored fluorescent tubes in a plaza in Manhattan's financial district, it was twice published in the *New York Times*, including a front-page photograph on December 17, 1997. But Smith says the real breakthrough in his practice came at the turn of the century, when he was working on the renovation of Lever House with David Childs of Skidmore, Owings & Merrill. Research on the landscape beneath the landmark Gordon Bunshaft building, including into sculptor Isamu Noguchi's unrealized plans for the site, led to the restoration of the plaza as it had been built in 1952, with some additions from the Noguchi proposal. It also led to what Smith terms more "establishment" work for him, notably urban plazas at 55 Water Street and 7 World Trade Center, the latter again with David Childs of SOM.

Accelerating work led to a growing office: after having just a small staff in the 1990s, including Elizabeth Asawa and YoonChul Cho, he hired a string of other talented designers in the early years of this decade, including Judith Wong, Annie Weinmayr, Hardy Stecker, Tobias Armborst, Christian Gabriel, Yvi Nguyen, and Alexander Felson, the last also an ecologist. He has typically employed between eight and ten people since then and recently established an office in Southern California to manage the Orange County Great Park.

In the quest to make sense of Smith's work, it might also help to know how he himself has presented it over the years. A 1996 exhibition, "Relics, Prosthetics, and Surrogates," revolved around his infatuation with simulation and substitution—the replacement of the "natural" with the "artificial" in particular. Smith subsequently delivered a series of lectures with titles that confirmed the range of his intellectual and artistic ambitions. "Transgressive Landscapes" presented his art installations of the late 1990s, which he says involved "applying something in the wrong place in the wrong way," like putting chandeliers on Fifth Avenue, costuming people as garden daisies or topiary for photographic montages, or nesting them naked as Adam and Eve in a room filled with plastic flowers and fruit at the budget tourist Hotel Eden. "Urban Projects," from the early 2000s, revealed how the provocateur could put on a public face and

make a beneficial mark on the city, as at Harlem Gateway/Malcolm X Plaza, Lever House, or P.S. 19, all in New York. "No Bushes," from the era of George the 43rd, was an obvious political dig; it also took aim at stereotypes of the profession—often regarded as little more than the art of placing shrubs around a building.

Most recently, "Big, Little, Skip the Middle" continues his critique of landscape architecture. The title refers to his preferred mode of working: a big concept finished with good detail. But it also expresses his aversion to the middle of the professional road. "The middle is standard practice—serving the client, picking stuff out of catalogs, solving program. I want a critical practice—a practice that tries to change practice." Notions of critical practice are confoundingly elastic—even elusive—and Smith is no better and no worse than most of his contemporaries in defining it. That said, he certainly conveys in his lectures, writings, and public comments a self-consciousness about his work and its relation to larger cultural discourses, along with a degree of skepticism about the usual standards of practice.

Although he runs the risk of having at least some of his work dismissed as fun, decorative, or witty—"I don't have to wear a hair shirt," he insists—he has clearly positioned himself between the more experimental world of installation art and the more normative world of landscape architecture.

The irony is that Smith has recently been starting to cloak himself in outwardly normative dress. In the Santa Fe Railyard Park, for instance, Smith engaged with the familiar typology of an urban park at a medium scale—one kind of middle that he might have avoided. But with artist Mary Miss and architect Frederic Schwartz, he took on the project and did it exceedingly well. Starting in 2002, a careful analysis of the 13-acre site revealed layers of cultural history, including an abandoned nineteenth-century rail yard and a section of a 400-year-old irrigation canal, the Acequia Madre; these would provide the two main spatial orders for the park. Many of its principal features are strung out along the remains of an old narrow-gauge line, where an overlay of circles contains program elements like playgrounds and picnic areas; this spine also provides links to neighborhood cultural institutions and a farmers market. If the rail line and canal provide the organizational structure for the park, water provides the narrative. The Acequia Madre is used to irrigate a demonstration vegetable garden; storm water is captured from nearby rooftops and stored in a prominent new tank in the park's main plaza. From here, drip fountains lead to a ceremonial watershed map as well as to diverse xeriscape plantings, native grasses, and an apricot orchard. These plantings constitute a third order for the park. Some of them are regional—a cottonwood bosque along the acequia, for instance, or plantings of piñon pine in an arroyo. But some of them Smith describes as "cultural plantings"—neither native nor xeric, but plants that have a long history of use in local gardens, like roses, sedums, and hollyhocks. Smith's attention to the cultural value of plants in community history is an expression of the extensive public review required by this project. In addition to participating in workshops and open houses to discern community ambitions for the park, Smith was involved in outreach and fundraising for the Trust for Public Land, which managed the project for the city of Santa Fe.

If Smith's work in Santa Fe is normative in some respects, it is decidedly not in others. It is especially unusual in the way he deploys ecosystem units, whether arroyo, bosque, or native grasses: the units are organized into distinctive patches, almost like the modules of minimalist sculpture. Smith's organization of ecological systems into an organic patchwork can be traced back to his work in Toronto, where the Village of Yorkville Park is a sequence of different ecosystems collaged together and presented almost like a cabinet of curiosities. Filled with evocations of different landscape types—pine groves, prairies, alder woods—they are organized into linear subdivisions that correspond to the property lines of adjacent row houses. One of the patches features a massive piece of local granite taken apart along existing fractures and reassembled on site, recapitulating the pulling apart and putting together that characterizes the park's larger design. As Alex Felson observes, Smith perceives ecosystems not only in terms of function but also as elements that can be deployed singly or in sequence for aesthetic effect.

Smith pulled off this strategy nicely in Toronto and again at a larger scale in Santa Fe. He is now attempting it at the regional scale in his proposal for the Orange County Great Park, which will include a restored stream and floodplains along with replanted orange groves. Its most audacious element may well be a 2.5-mile canyon that will be newly created for the park. It will feature palms and other plantings along a watercourse some 60 feet deep, to be created by digging down 30 feet and piling the material 30 feet high on either side of the excavation. The canyon is rooted, Smith says, in "natural archetypes" like the palm canyons of Palm Springs or Balboa Park in San Diego. But it will be entirely synthetic: it will be fed with water recycled from an existing sewage treatment plant at the head of the canyon. The water will be discharged into four or five acres of treatment wetlands; it will then enter the canyon, a self-contained watershed that will terminate in a 24-acre lake. From there, water

John Beardsley

will be drawn to irrigate the remainder of the park. Smith says he is using "natural typologies as a reference and doing them in a more constructed way at larger scale." In this, he is harkening back to some of his earliest work, particularly the exhibition "Relics, Prosthetics, and Surrogates." The stream is distinctly prosthetic; it is also a kind of simulacrum—an evocation of an original that never existed on the site.

The "camouflage garden" for the roof of the Museum of Modern Art reminds us that however normative his work might look at times, Smith remains an experimenter and provocateur at heart, much like the artists he admires. The MoMA garden, intended as a temporary installation, was a simulation both pragmatic and aesthetic: weight issues and desiccating winds contributed to the decision to use only artificial materials on the roof. Some of them are even recycled, including black "beach pebbles" made from shredded tires. ("Sustainable design doesn't have to wear its ideology on its sleeve," Smith says.) Despite its imagery, the garden is anything but camouflaged. Although it can be viewed only from above, it screams its presence to those who can see it, much like the hip-hop camo pants it is meant to suggest. Moreover, Smith's use of color is as experimental as his use of materials. While color selection at MoMA was governed by the source material, Smith can use it in ways that range from subtle to screeching: diagonal drifts of muted pinks and lavender in the Sagaponack garden, diagonal bands of vivid pink and white azaleas at 7 World Trade Center. At a still louder end, he painted polka dots in blue, teal, orange, and pink all over the walls and grounds of a children's play area at P.S. 19; bright orange appears again almost as a branding device at the Orange County Preview Park.

Smith's analogies to the fashion house raise two final questions: Can his label outlast him? Is there a wider future for his particular lines of work? He could certainly nurture younger talents to carry on his lines, as other firms have done before him. But even if his particular modes of expression remain only and obdurately his, he offers a glimpse of a kind of practice that ought to inspire others. It is one of great flexibility and versatility, one that questions received ways of thinking and making, one that is not afraid to reinvent itself as opportunities arise or occasions require. In questioning his own assumptions and the habits of the profession, he offers one model of a critical practice. Whether or not we can fully comprehend or even appreciate what on earth he is up to, Ken Smith injects an element of experimentation into a profession that all too often can seem all too conventionalized. For this, ladies and gentlemen, hats off to him—whatever fashion you profess.

John Beardsley is the director of garden and landscape studies at Dumbarton Oaks, Washington, D.C., and a senior lecturer in the Department of Landscape Architecture at the Harvard University Graduate School of Design.

John Beardsley

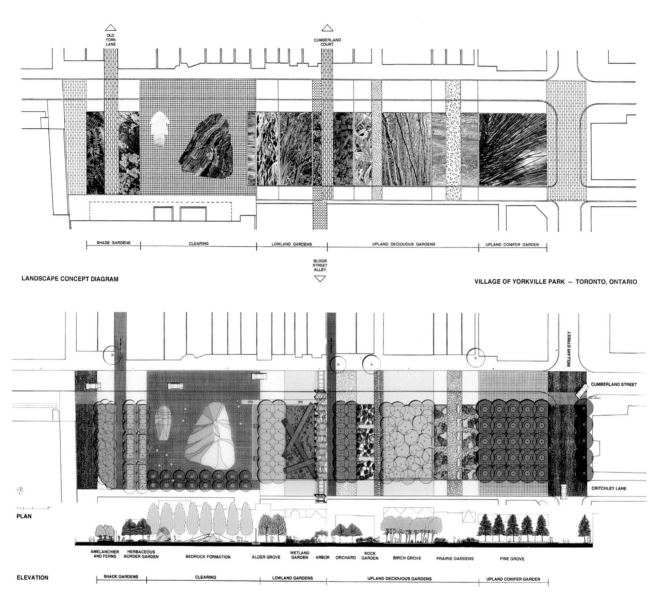

LANDSCAPE CONCEPT DIAGRAM

| SHADE GARDENS | CLEARING | LOWLAND GARDENS | UPLAND DECIDUOUS GARDENS | UPLAND CONIFER GARDEN |

OLD YORK LANE

CUMBERLAND COURT

BLOOR STREET ALLEY

VILLAGE OF YORKVILLE PARK -- TORONTO, ONTARIO

PLAN

ELEVATION

BELLAIR STREET

CUMBERLAND STREET

CRITCHLEY LANE

AMELANCHIER AND FERNS   HERBACEOUS BORDER GARDEN   BEDROCK FORMATION   ALDER GROVE   WETLAND GARDEN   ARBOR   ORCHARD   ROCK GARDEN   BIRCH GROVE   PRAIRIE GARDENS   PINE GROVE

| SHADE GARDENS | CLEARING | LOWLAND GARDENS | UPLAND DECIDUOUS GARDENS | UPLAND CONIFER GARDEN |

LANDSCAPE SCHEMATIC DESIGN

VILLAGE OF YORKVILLE PARK -- TORONTO, ONTARIO

VILLAGE OF YORK-VILLE PARK

Toronto, Ontario   1992–1994

This one-acre project was a transitional one for me. During my partnership with Martha Schwartz and David Meyer in San Francisco, I served as lead designer for our winning Yorkville competition entry. In 1992, when I left Martha Schwartz, Ken Smith, David Meyer to open my own practice, I carried the Yorkville project forward. I continued to work with David Meyer as we made site visits throughout the two-year installation process.

The idea of this urban park dates back to the late 1950s, when a block of Victorian-era row houses along Cumberland Street was demolished to allow for the construction of the Bloor-Danforth subway line. For years this highly visible site—between the small-scale old Yorkville neighborhood with its late-nineteenth- and early-twentieth-century row houses and the high-rise commercial core that has built up along the Bloor Street corridor since the subway opened—remained a parking lot. Activist neighbors fought to build a public place to bring the area together rather than to divide it. In 1991 the City of Toronto Department of Parks, Forestry & Recreation finally announced an international design competition.

The community wanted a park that would reflect the scale and context of the neighborhood, incorporate the ecology of the surrounding region, and make connections with the local streets and a system of midblock passageways. My strategy for the competition was to design the park to express the Victorian style of collecting. In this case, we were "collecting" the landscapes of Ontario—pine groves, prairies, marshes, orchards, alder woods, rock outcroppings, and so on—and arranging them in the scale and pattern of the nineteenth-century row house lot lines.

The park design creates a series of linear subdivisions that align with the property boundaries across the street and connect to the nearby midblock passageways. Each linear park segment is distinct in character but related to the next, creating a park of diversity and unity. To anchor the space with an element of regional glacial geology, we arranged for a 700-ton bedrock outcrop of native Muskoka granite to be taken apart along natural crevices, moved 150 miles south, and reconstructed on-site. Immense yet inviting, the outcrop has a wonderful tactile surface for sitting, and it absorbs warmth on cool sunny days. Movable tables and chairs next to the boulder suggest a contrast between permanence and flexibility.

While small in size, Yorkville's park has become a local landmark. Popular and well used, it has played an important role in the revitalization of the neighborhood since its completion in 1994. I've been back to visit a number of times in the years since. Despite some recent restoration work, its original design integrity as a distillation of regional ecology, along with its role as a neighborhood connection point, remains as strong as ever.

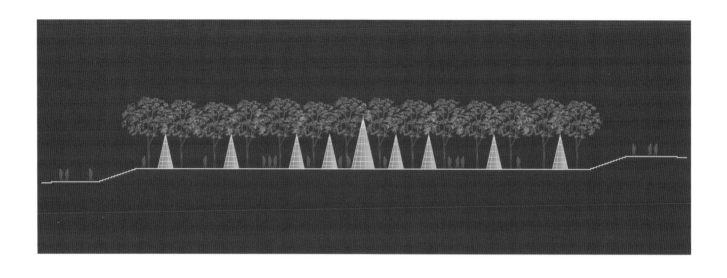

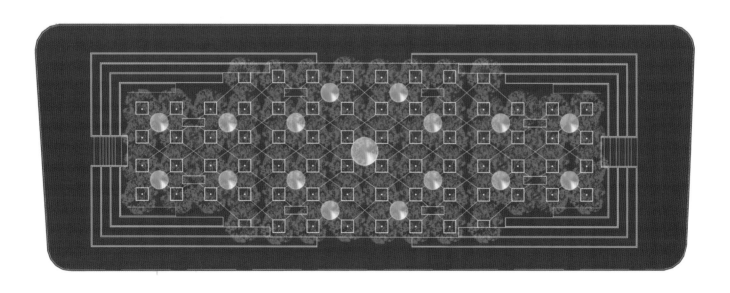

GLOWING TOPIARY GARDEN

New York, New York 1997

One of my first realized public projects in New York City was a two-month installation at Liberty Plaza in the Financial District. Designed to bring color and light to dark winter nights, this garden transformed an ordinary hardscape plaza into an ephemeral oasis with the calm of a Zen monastery and the sculptural precision of a French topiary garden.

Installed in time for the 1997 winter solstice, the Glowing Topiary Garden lasted through the brief holiday season, bringing mystery and pleasure to the shortest days of the year. I collaborated with lighting designer Jim Conti, the first of our many partnerships. We placed sixteen 16-foot tall topiary cones, manufactured using the materials and techniques of standard commercial backlit vinyl awnings, over the existing grid of "lollipop" mercury-vapor lampposts in the plaza. One 24-foot-tall cone at the center provided a sense of focus. The large cone-shaped lanterns formed a garden space in the midst of a crowded urban setting.

We added fluorescent bulbs with theater gels to the base of the cones, creating the effect of white light at the top of the cone and colored light at the ground. Eight of the cones near the installation's center were equipped with electronic sound devices that created an acoustic space. In addition, we placed 250 wind chimes throughout the canopy of locust trees to create air music for a pervasive soundscape effect.

Our intention was to express the whole space of Liberty Plaza and to reveal qualities inherent to the place but often unnoticed or unappreciated. The topiary cones and the light spaces they created could be seen simultaneously in the background and the foreground; they were capable of accommodating many levels of attention and interpretation without highlighting any one element. The movement of people walking through the space added vitality of motion and randomness to the stationary cones and

lights. As they explored, visitors experienced spatial shifts in color and sound moving from east to west and north to south.

Together, the sculpted forms, sounds,

and light environment created an ambient landscape that became a world in itself. The time of day or night affected visitors' color perceptions, just as the sounds of the city affected their absorption in the project's sound environment. With a limited material palette and minimalist geometry, we achieved a changing and immersive space of enclosure. No matter what the hour, it brought visitors a feeling of serenity and a space in the heart of the city to think and reflect.

New York, New York   1997

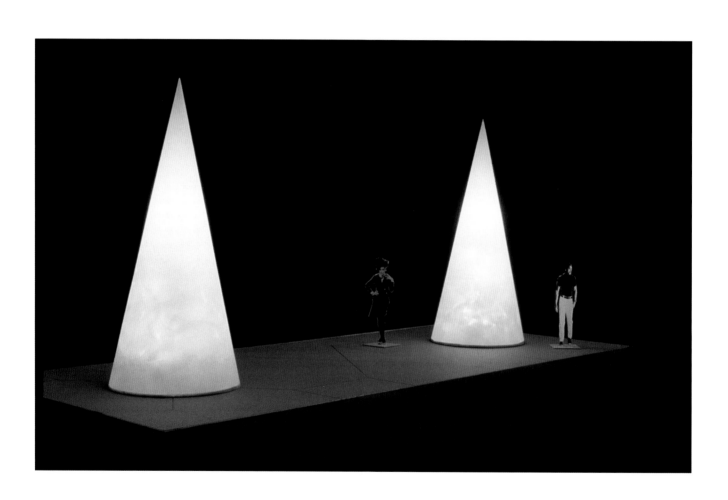

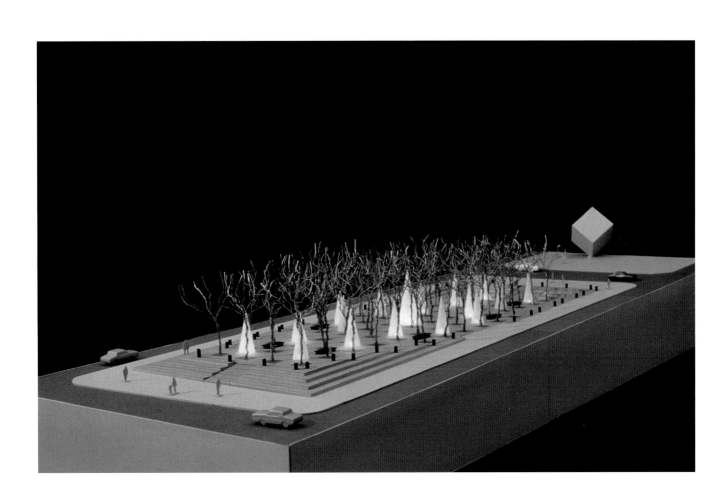

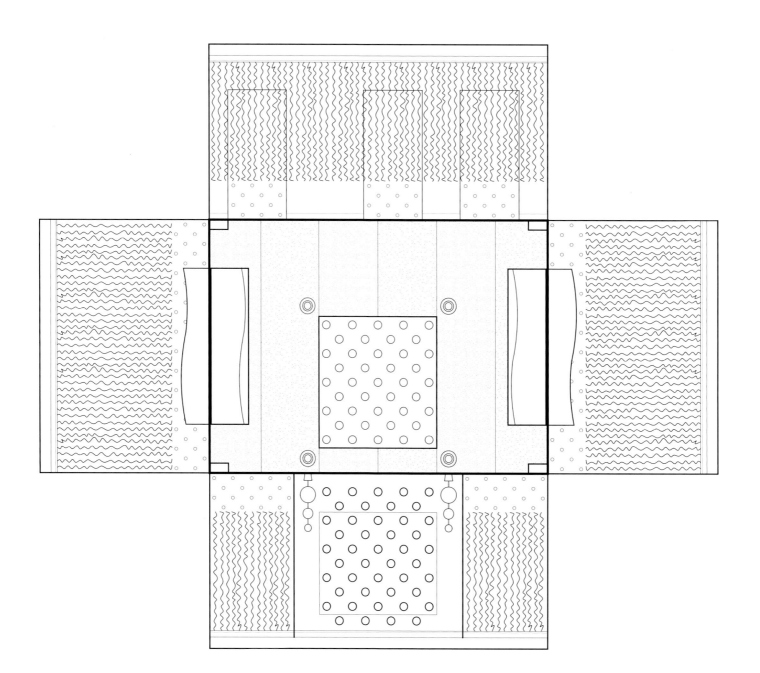

HOTEL EDEN

New York, New York   2000

The 1990s were a period of experimentation for me. I began to receive small commissions and take part in temporary art projects and competitions. Through my teaching, I was beginning to explore ideas that would shape my later work, such as the difference between "sites" and "nonsites," simulation and appropriation, systems of order and their deployment, materiality and fabrication. I did an installation, Garden Deities, in 1997 and a series of photomontages, Hair Gardens, in 1998. I was also beginning to explore ideas of vertical landscape architecture. I had few paying commissions and very little money, and many of my projects from this time explored how to create landscapes in opportunistic situations or with found or inexpensive objects. The dumpster gardens I proposed for Queens Plaza are an example of this approach.

In late 1999, I was commissioned by *Nest*

magazine to create a garden installation in a hotel room for the summer 2000 issue. I chose the smallest budget-tourist room at the Roger Smith Hotel near Grand Central Station as the site. Inside room 401, I worked for several weeks to craft an indoor garden from simulated flowers and artificial land- scape materials. The idea was to "plant" a new kind of Garden of Eden in which a young couple would live in an oasis of respite from the winter city.

We decorated the ceiling with 700 silk calla lilies, rolled out a smooth lawn of arti- ficial turf on the floor, and hand-sewed a comforter of spandex camouflage fabric decorated with large artificial sunflowers and plastic frogs. The walls were covered with plastic vines dripping with miniature plastic apples, lemons, and oranges. Anthropologist Tobias Schneebaum visited the couple well into their weeklong stay, as they sat on the comforter naked with their legs entwined. He noted how when they moved, the plastic frogs in the comforter squeaked like a child's toy: "The whole effect was not only amusing—it also put into perspective the difference between art and pure decoration."

Coming into their paradise from the outside, Schneebaum suspected that going "back to nature" in this pocket world may have somehow changed the young man and woman. "There was a gentleness about them

LEVER HOUSE

New York, New York   1999–2002

In the late 1990s, I became involved in preservation efforts aimed at built landscapes of the modern era, many of which remain threatened with neglect or outright demolition. I researched the work of Dan Kiley at Lincoln Center and Lawrence Halprin in Rochester, New York. Partly as a result of my personal interest in preservation, I was commissioned to work on the restoration of Lever House, the modern curtain-wall landmark designed in the early 1950s by Gordon Bunshaft of Skidmore, Owings & Merrill. By this time, the landscape at Lever House had been quite altered, and little was known about the original design.

One fascinating part of the story is that during SOM's construction document phase for Lever House, Bunshaft collaborated with Isamu Noguchi on an ambitious landscape scheme that was never realized. With the assistance of landscape architect Gavin Keeney, I researched the SOM archive at Columbia University's Avery Library and the Lever House project archives at the Noguchi Foundation. But sorting through the design's complex history and evolution was only the beginning of the restoration effort. We also needed to seek approvals and to work with many players, including the building owner, SOM, the Noguchi Foundation, and the New York City Landmarks Preservation Commission.

Lever House features an innovative open ground-floor plan with a plaza, garden courtyard, and small glass-enclosed lobby. The second and third floors appear to float over the street and act as a base for the slender glass tower. Open to the street, the garden built in 1952 was similar to model photos published in 1950. Although there were not many drawings of the landscape design in the SOM archives, the landscape was well documented in a series of photographs taken by Ezra Stoller at the completion of construction and during the first few years of the building's life.

Our task involved restoring the landscape to its as-built condition (based largely on the Stoller photos) with some plant material adjustments. We substituted a sculptural Japanese maple for the original weeping willow tree that hadn't survived the limited light conditions of the courtyard site. We restored the original hedge plinth that went from outside to inside along with the podium-level perimeter hedge and locust tree plantings. I added an azalea garden under the trees.

Working with art consultant Richard Marshall and the Isamu Noguchi Foundation, we incorporated a number of Noguchi sculptures, on a five-year loan from the foundation, into the landscape design. The project also involved fabricating and installing marble seating designed for the plaza by Noguchi but never installed.

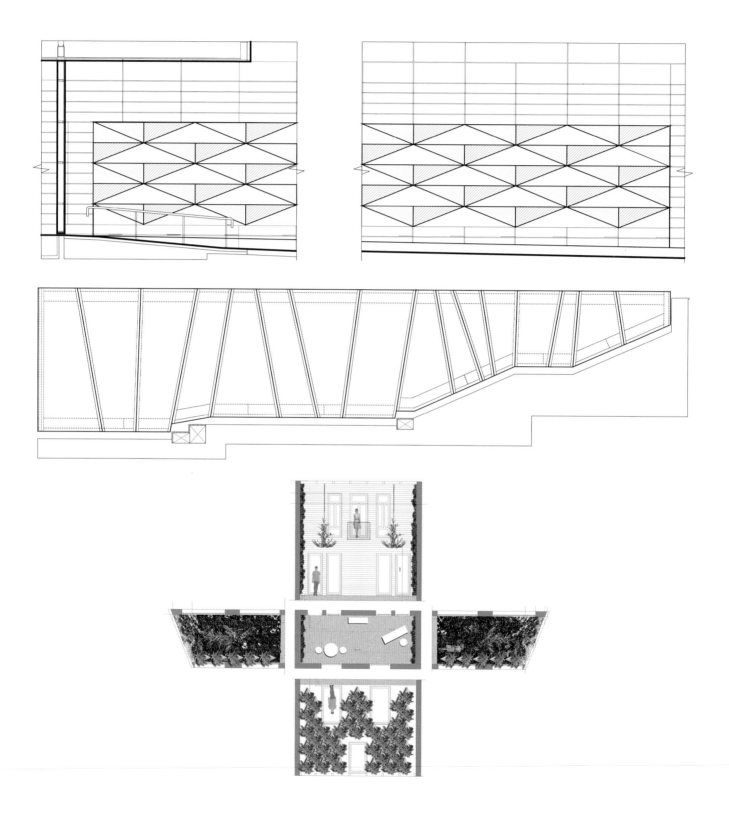

FOUR VERTICAL GARDENS

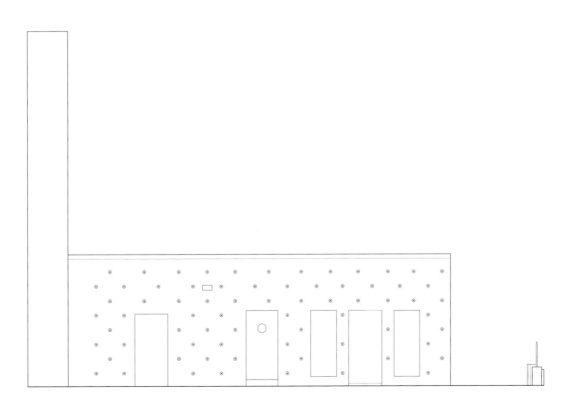

New York, New York   1999–2005

In June 2001, I wrote a short polemic for the newsletter of the Architectural League of New York in which I stated, "With horizontal space at a premium, New York City buildings have traditionally exploited vertical space. As the contested ground plane limits New Yorkers' access to gardens and green space, it is time to address the obvious solution of vertical gardens. Building gardens and open landscape space into the vertical structure of every new building in the city will provide greater access to green space. I imagine a profusion of sky gardens, facade topiaries, hanging parterres, aerial *allées* and embedded *orangeries*. It is time to create a more integrated cohabitation of landscape and architecture in the city."

I have been interested in the notion of vertical landscapes for some time, as seen in Hotel Eden and the WallFlowers project at the Cooper-Hewitt, National Design Museum. The principles of vertical planting are ancient, expressing traditions ranging from Mesopotamian hanging gardens to French topiary. They can include vines and other species that are highly shade tolerant and well suited for "urban horticulture" on rooftops and in small spaces. In recent years, I have proposed a number of vertical landscapes. For the most part they are unrealized, except for these four, which are both inside and outside, both public and private.

Time Warner Center
For the residential tower of the Time Warner Center, I designed a folded topiary with a sculpted structure fabricated of stainless steel. The five rows of triangular planters are filled with *Euonymus* and *Vinca minor*, hardy vines that soften the entry and grow down in a cascading form. The ground planter beneath the topiary wall is planted with Korean boxwood.

Milan Condominium

In the interior courtyard of a high-rise residential building, I created a garden with a folded topiary wall consisting of a stainless-steel frame and expanded steel mesh. The wall is covered with English ivy. An off-center paved path runs in perspective to a folded metal staircase of diamond tread plate. On the way, visitors pass two wood steps painted with an aluminum stain that I developed. Deep in the garden is a bamboo grove that grows well in its sheltered setting.

Atrium Courtyard

In this 9-by-22-foot skylit atrium of an old firehouse, I designed a wall garden of hanging tropical plantings. The floor of the garden is made of shredded recycled rubber, a pervious material that is water and humidity tolerant. The walls are studded with off-the-shelf modern classic ceramic planters suspended in thin stainless-steel pot rings that I designed to fit the matte-finish pots. The rings install easily into the grouting of the existing brick.

Sutton Place Penthouse

This New York roof terrace of several hundred square feet is a serene home for Jeff Koons's well-known sculpture *Green Diamond*. We devised a circular Corian base for the piece and placed it for optimal viewing from both inside and out. Originally it had been displayed in Basel on a rectangular base, but for this small rooftop terrace, the circular form allowed for nondirectional and fluid circulation around the diamond. On the east wall, I created a WallFlower installation of synthetic purple daisies in PVC "plant-flanges" in a diamond pattern.

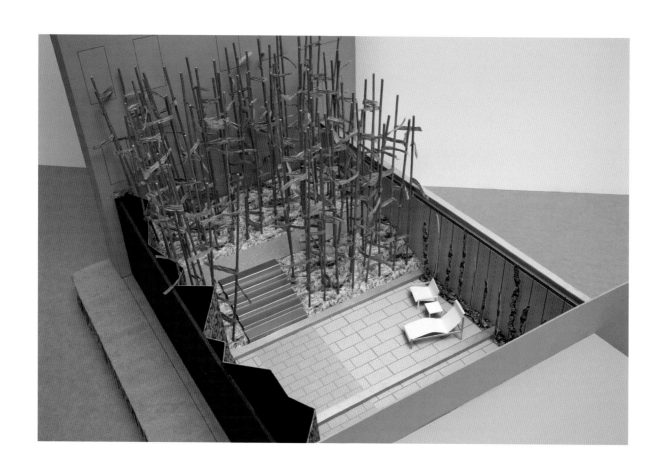

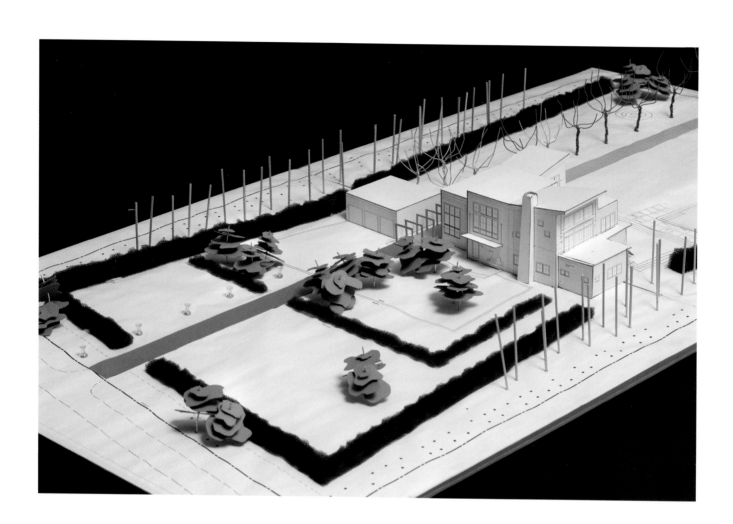

SAGA-PONACK RESI-DENCE

Sagaponack, New York   2001–2002

I have always admired the essential flatness of landscapes in the Hamptons. I am drawn to the open views and to how generations of residents developed a language of immense privet hedges to foster privacy. In 2001 I had a chance to work with the light and ecology of the Hamptons at a two-acre site for a summer home redesigned by architect Karen Jacobson. In a historic landscape that looks out to the sea and sky, it makes sense to create frames of trees, hedges, and arbors that heighten their impressive scale.

True to form for the Hamptons, this project's oblong site is nearly flat, located on former Long Island potato fields, with conservation easements preserving the views on either end. I decided to draw on the local vernacular of flat ground planes and linear three-dimensional hedges and windrows in my design. The landscape plan highlights the protected long views at the northeast and

Sagaponack Residence

southwest ends of the site while screening out the neighboring houses on the sides.

Like an hourglass, the plan is subtly pinched at the center—adjacent to the house—to create an enhanced sense of perspective and an expanded sense of space. By slightly angling the hedges at the sides, we crafted wedge-shaped spaces along the lot lines for taller privacy plantings of ornamental understory trees.

I created the frame of hedges using inkberry and hydrangea, giving the border both evergreen and seasonal flowers. An L-shaped herbaceous garden frames the entry court with dunelike drifts of perennials, including yarrow, sagebrush, lavender, Nippon daisy, and perennial sage. To contrast with the lines of hedges, gardens, and trees, I placed Hollywood junipers in seemingly random patterns around the entry court. Their sculptural branch forms provide year-round color and texture and also echo the angled profile of the house's rooflines.

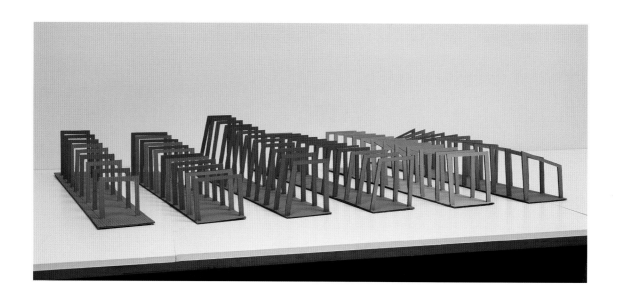

Between the house and garage, a central axis of wood planks acts as a bridge that connects the long views. Near the middle of this axis, we built an arbor of heavy-gauge aluminum and wood with inserts of frosted acrylic and planted it with wisteria. To heighten the drama of the axis, I designed the arbor with an altered perspective. At one end, the frame is a square of 8 by 8 feet; the space tapers to a rectangle of 8 by 12 feet.

Sagaponack Residence

The framing poles have a graduated spacing that complements this perspectival effect. To emphasize the central axis as it continues outward to the northeast vista, we planted a special "bionic turf" of highly fertilized grass; this is brighter and left slightly taller than the mowed grass around it.

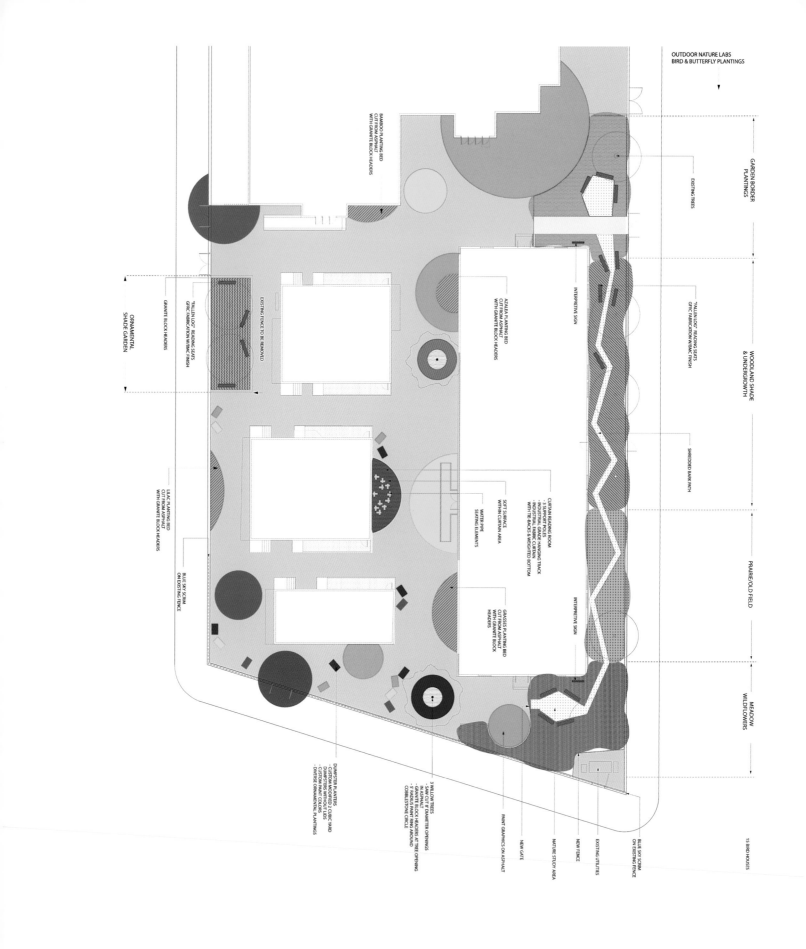

OUTDOOR NATURE LABS
BIRD & BUTTERFLY PLANTINGS

GARDEN BORDER PLANTINGS

WOODLAND SHADE & UNDERGROWTH

PRAIRIE/OLD FIELD

MEADOW WILDFLOWERS

15 BIRD HOUSES

EXISTING TREES

"FALLEN LOG" READING SEATS
GFRC FABRICATION W/BMC FINISH

SHREDDED BARK PATH

INTERPRETIVE SIGN

BLUE SKY SCRIM
ON EXISTING FENCE

EXISTING UTILITIES

NEW FENCE

NATURE STUDY AREA

NEW GATE

PAINT GRAPHICS ON ASPHALT

3 WILLOW TREES
- SAW CUT 6' DIAMETER OPENINGS
  IN ASPHALT
- GRANITE BLOCK HEADERS AT TREE OPENING
- 5' RADIUS PAINT RING AROUND
- COBBLESTONE CIRCLE

DUMPSTER PLANTERS
- CUSTOM MODIFIED 2 CUBIC YARD
  DUMPSTERS WITHOUT LIDS
- CUSTOM PAINT COLORS
- DIVERSE ORNAMENTAL PLANTINGS

LILAC PLANTING BED
CUT FROM ASPHALT
WITH GRANITE BLOCK HEADERS

BLUE SKY SCRIM
ON EXISTING FENCE

GRANITE BLOCK HEADERS

ORNAMENTAL
SHADE GARDEN

EXISTING FENCE TO BE REMOVED

"FALLEN LOG" READING SEATS
GFRC FABRICATION W/BMC FINISH

BAMBOO PLANTING BED
CUT FROM ASPHALT
WITH GRANITE BLOCK HEADERS

AZALEA PLANTING BED
CUT FROM ASPHALT
WITH GRANITE BLOCK HEADERS

WATER PIPE
SEATING ELEMENTS

SOFT SURFACE
WITHIN CURTAIN AREA

CURTAIN READING ROOM
- 3 SUPPORT POLES
- INDUSTRIAL GRADE HANGING TRACK
- INDUSTRIAL GRADE FABRIC CURTAIN
  WITH TIE-BACKS & WEIGHTED BOTTOM

INTERPRETIVE SIGN

GRASSES PLANTING BED
CUT FROM ASPHALT
WITH GRANITE BLOCK
HEADERS

P.S. 19

Queens, New York   2002–2003

P.S. 19 was a pro bono project for the Robin Hood Foundation's Library Initiative, a program that engages architects to design school libraries for New York City's poorest neighborhoods. This schoolyard, the first landscape project commissioned by the foundation, gave us the opportunity to bring a new sense of pride, color, and playfulness to the barren asphalt spaces woven through the school's classroom buildings, "temporary" structures that have been in use for 20 years.

I conceived the project as a set of five prototypes, each addressing a typical schoolyard problem: forbidding fence, ubiquitous asphalt paving, lack of furnishings, scarcity of green space, and limited areas for kids and classes to gather together for reading and learning. In the first phase, we applied bright round graphics to the standardized steel classroom buildings. On the pavement, we used similar polka dots of color to roll out a "graphic carpet" that incorporates reflective glass beads, like those used in city crosswalks, to add sparkle to particular areas of the pattern.

We scattered rolling dumpsters, custom-sized so the kids could reach them, near water faucets around the site. Initially, we were not sure how the kids and teachers would react to these "dumpster gardens." When I went back to visit, I discovered that the teachers reserved them for their classes by painting a number on the front. The kids eagerly took on projects in their adopted dumpsters—and there's a great deal of change and variety.

The Bird and Butterfly Garden was planted by volunteers on Earth Day in 2003, the second year. It is the most beloved part of the garden, a place where kids sit alone and read, and classes study the plants and insects while also making plantings of their own. We planted hardy colorful perennials, including lily, hollyhock, bishop's weed, butterfly bush, daffodil, and snowberry.

The project is filled with common materials used in new ways. For example, I proposed an outdoor reading room ringed by orange construction netting. Its webbed pattern defined a special place yet kept it visually open. Kids and teachers could slide the netting back on its hanging rod to transform the space for different kinds of activity. Although this feature was never installed, I brought some very large logs to the site and arranged them to create defined spaces for sitting and reading.

To enliven the chain-link fence, we introduced a sense of color and sky with a long "cloud scrim" panorama printed on industrial fabric. It raises the eye to an always-blue horizon that is visible from both the street and inside the garden. The banner is the most ephemeral part of the project, because the material only lasts about five years. But because it was inexpensive—commercially inkjet-printed on fabric that comes in large rolls—it should be easy to reproduce and replace if the school chooses. P.S. 19 shows that we can achieve socially responsible city parks and great design at the same time. If we look beyond typical off-the-shelf benches, play structures, and planters, it is possible to reimagine everyday city objects and spaces as opportunities for wonder.

55
WATER
STREET

New York, New York   2002–2005

Manhattan is an island with surprisingly few views of the rivers that surround it—especially in the Wall Street area, where the city began. The winning entry in a competition sponsored by the Municipal Art Society, this one-acre park renews a 1960s-era plaza set on a podium 30 feet above street level. The challenges of the site were many, and I collaborated with Rogers Marvel Architects to integrate the existing office buildings with a vision for a softer and more inviting "elevated acre." We needed to improve the stair/escalator connection to Water Street and to serve a variety of public needs and activities, including quiet places to enjoy the view and comfortable seating and grass areas to enjoy lunch. We also needed to program larger spaces for outdoor performances and organized events.

My primary concern was to create a landscape that was lightweight enough to be built over a parking garage yet lush enough to be satisfying as a park. The design vocabulary is rooted in an abstraction of the terminal moraine dunescape that historically typifies the geology of the area and has a visual relationship to the harbor. My strategy was to tilt the ground plane and create a series of landscape "dunes" with plantings. Dunes and paved areas run in long parallel segments set across the sloped space. Visitors approach the river along an angled path that passes through the dunes.

Working in three dimensions, the design manipulates perspective, with the sloping hill initially obscuring the view of the East River and the harbor. As visitors traverse the slope, the horizon gradually opens up and the East River, the graceful span of the Brooklyn Bridge, and the harbor are dramatically revealed. I designed a paving system of concrete planks to create an "interdigitated" edge that weaves together the interlocking layers of hard and soft landscapes. The dunes are planted with a scattered canopy of locust trees; on the landward slopes are woodland plantings, including white rhododendron and arrowwood viburnum, and on the more exposed harbor sides are ornamental grasses and wildflowers, such as maiden grass, *Pennisetum*, and black-eyed Susan.

Inserted next to the planted dunes are wood benches punctuated with metal seat-backs. The wood slats of the benches and the parallel concrete planks recall beach boardwalks running through the dunes. A slightly raised lawn and stepped seating on the northern edge of the plaza supports performances and group events. The oasis of the lawn also serves as a place for informal activities, such as picnics and reading the newspaper. An illuminated beacon at one corner gives the plaza visibility and prominence from the street.

Even though the park is still elevated, it no longer seems disconnected from its context and the life of the city. With the East River as a backdrop and a view of the historic ships moored at the South Street Seaport, there's a rediscovered sense here of the ocean and the harbor shipping that helped to build New York.

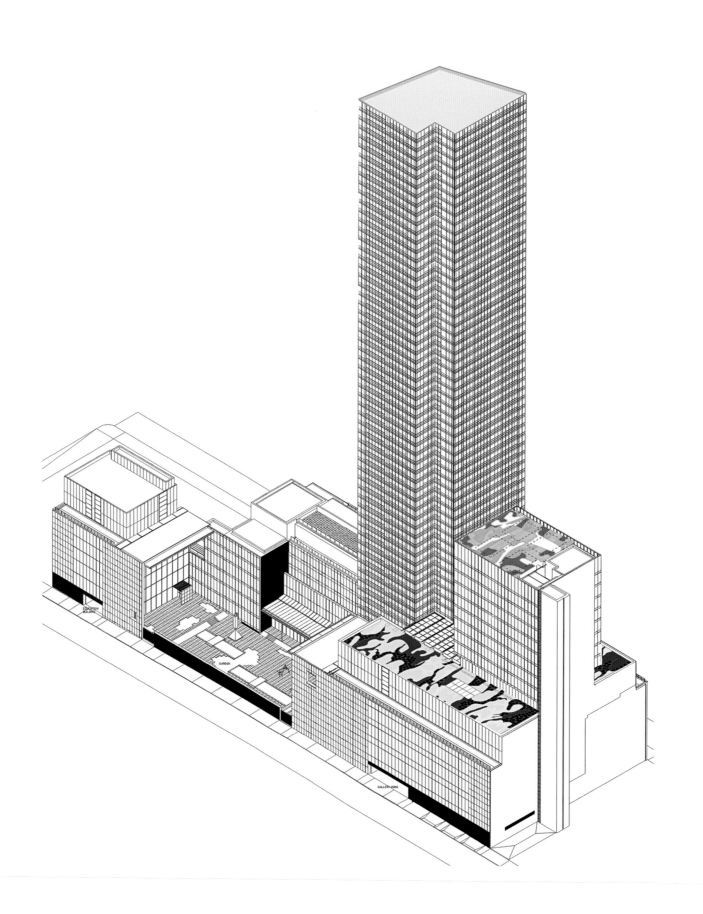

MoMA ROOF GARDEN

New York, New York   2002–2005

For the new roof garden at the MoMA, I explored the idea of simulated nature and the strategies of camouflage to create a lightweight, low-maintenance rooftop garden. While it is very visible from surrounding buildings, the garden is physically inaccessible to visitors and very difficult to maintain with living plantings. For this reason, the solution needed to be durable, affordable, and hardy. We had to make a roof garden that was not a "garden" in the traditional sense of a terrace for gatherings, sculptures, and verdant trees. In other words, our challenge was to design a roof that did not look like a roof but openly disguised it with something new.

I've long been intrigued by landscape architecture as "camouflage." Disguising a site is so much a part of the history of our profession, although landscape architects rarely admit it. Camouflage, in its most utilitarian form, conceals by simulating the patterns and colors of natural forms. Many landscape architecture projects "shrub up" a place that is not "green enough" or create topography where there is none. For MoMA, I took the art of camouflage and the artifice of simulated nature a step further by making the strategies obvious. I used the idea of simulation itself as a source of appropriation and manipulation. The garden responds ironically to traditional applications of camouflage by simultaneously concealing the museum roof and drawing attention to it, by manipulating scale relationships, and by drawing into question the use of natural and artificial materials.

Curator Peter Reed, in his essay for the museum's 2005 "Groundswell" exhibition, observed, "Not only is [the roof garden] a simulation of real plants and rocks but it is also a subversion of camouflage's function to hide or conceal. Far from camouflaging the institution, the garden trumpets the Museum's location to all those who gaze down upon it." Reed also described the design's critique of traditional landscape architecture's complicity in covering up and hiding abused landscapes, such as sanitary landfills, old industrial sites, mines, and rail yards.

In fact, we were able to use recycled materials that might otherwise have ended up in one of those landfills. Originally, Yoshio Taniguchi Architects called for black Mexican beach pebbles for some of the surfaces. Our contractor suggested that shredded old rubber tires would be much less expensive and lighter in weight. We used many other materials—crushed glass, PVC pipes as stems for the plastic boxwood shrubs—rarely seen in public gardens. The boulders are actually the hollow plastic rocks that adorn suburban yards. The crushed white stone is the only natural material in the garden, although it is an open question how "natural" or manu-factured it really is. Whether the crushed glass in the blue surfaces is natural or syn-thetic may also be debated. Throughout, I tried to be honest about our simulation of nature's curves and our strategy of camou-flage. It makes sense that we didn't take our curving lines and shapes from a tradition-ally "natural" site, such as a field or forest. Instead, all the arcs, tangents, and straight lines in the plan are traced directly from the camouflage pattern in a pair of hip-hop skateboarder pants.

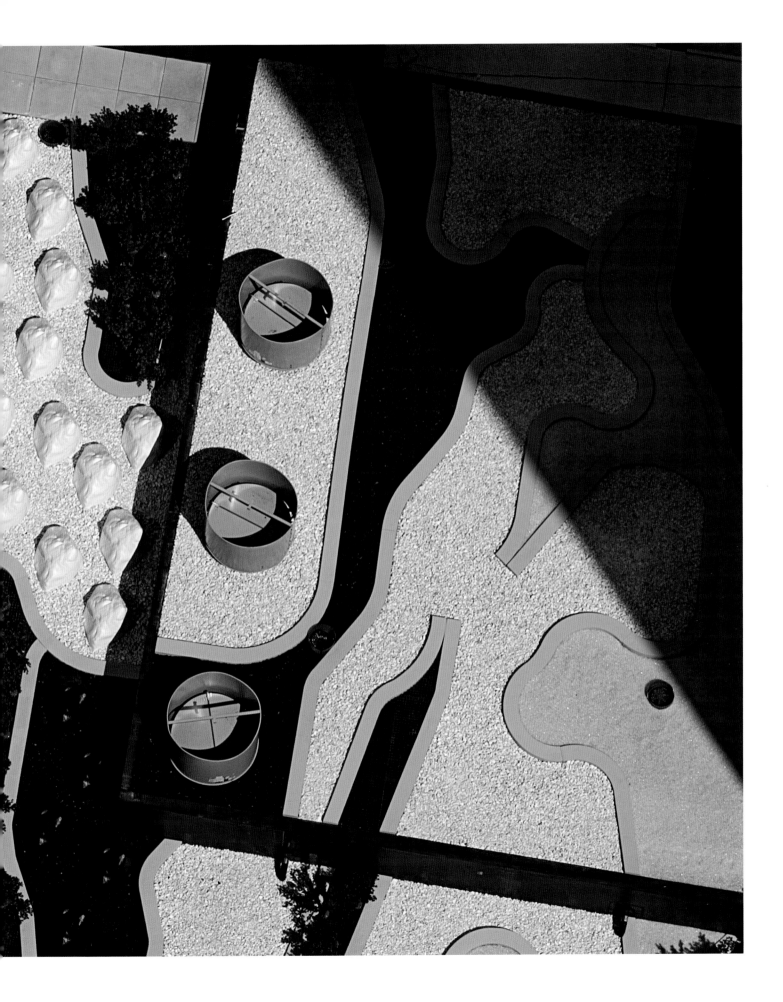

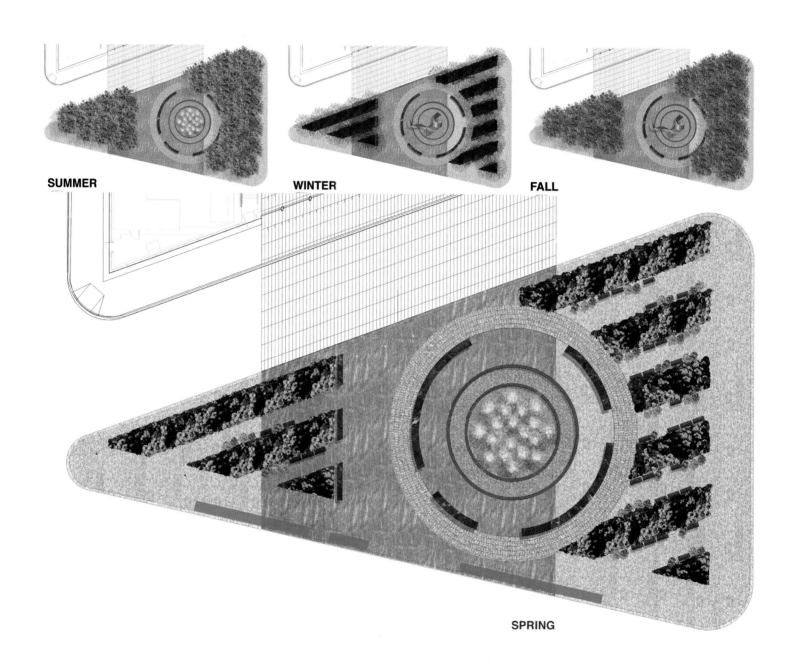

SUMMER

WINTER

FALL

SPRING

7 WORLD TRADE CENTER TRIANGLE PARK

New York, New York   2002–2006

I live and work in downtown New York, just a few blocks north of the World Trade Center. The vibrant urbanism of Lower Manhattan is fascinating because of its layered record of change, bursts of construction, subtractions, and new beginnings. Built in the early 1970s, partly on Hudson River landfill, the World Trade became a powerful American symbol and punctuation mark for Lower Manhattan. And then, in one morning, it was gone.

I was involved in the much-publicized World Trade Center redevelopment competition with Rafael Viñoly, Frederic Schwartz, Shigeru Ban, and the rest of the THINK Team when David Childs of Skidmore, Owings & Merrill invited me to work on the triangle park in front of the new 7 World Trade Center, which he was designing for developer Larry Silverstein. To respond to the trauma of the 9/11 terrorist attack, I felt the park needed to be a calm, carefully composed, and ordered place. Because the opening of the first new building at the World Trade Center site was so symbolically important, the tower and the park were both fast-track projects. Opened in spring 2006, the park's elegant simplicity and urbane materials belie a much more complicated below-ground infrastructure as well as myriad security concerns.

In planning the site, SOM advocated reopening Greenwich Street, a historic corridor closed years before. The extension of the street creates the triangular shape of the park and expresses the shifting grid of Lower Manhattan. I designed the park in response to the alignments of the triangular plot, with a classic three-part composition consisting of two tree groves flanking a central plaza with a fountain. The plaza and fountain sit on axis with the front lobby of the new building. Under the sweet gum trees in the flanking groves are linear gardens of boxwood and azalea, and between these bands are sheltered areas for seating and circulation. Although materials and geometry unify the park area, the composition of plaza and groves offers a set of distinctively scaled spaces that provide formality of entry and informality in social seating and pedestrian movement.

From the planting of the tightly spaced sweet gum trees to the proportions of the light fixtures and benches, the plaza is beautifully resolved in design details. After so much destruction and change on the site, I consciously chose materials that connote permanence and stability. Three kinds of stone are used in the central plaza. Robin Blue granite from Georgia lies at the base of the fountain waterspouts; gray Italian marble, which matches the stone in the building's lobby, forms the central carpet; the surfaces under the tree groves are paved with parallelogram sets of Rockville White granite. Because the ground plane is so important in such an urban space, I designed these parallelogram cobbles to bring the site's geometry, quite literally, down to earth. Stainless-steel headers contain the linear planting beds and contrast with the texture and coarseness of these pavers. Smooth bench arcs of Vermont Verde Antique marble, along with subtle stainless-steel lights, accentuate the fountain's circular form.

The park draws the new tower's lobby outward to daylight and open space. From the front doors, visitors see the park's two tree groves framing a WPA Moderne federal post office to the east. Seeking to create a sense of openness, we designed plantings and hardscape features to double as protective elements. Remarkably, in this most secure district, there are only two visible bollards in the park.

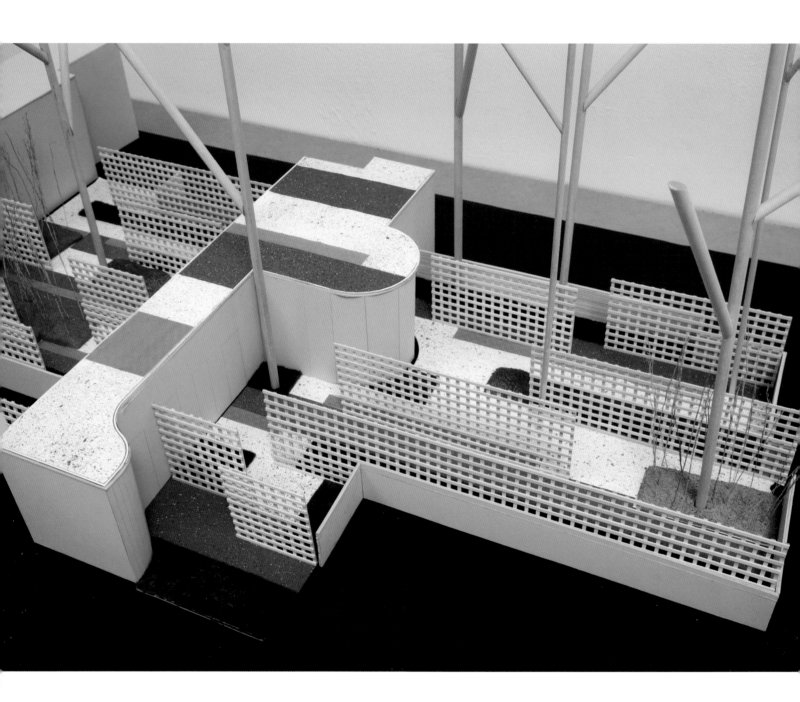

40 CENTRAL PARK SOUTH

New York, New York   2005–2006

Shortly after completing the rooftop garden at the MoMA, I was asked to design a small courtyard garden just south of Central Park. Set between two postwar apartment buildings facing Fifty-eighth and Fifty-ninth Streets, the garden has a material palette that is similar to MoMA's but without its irony and double entendre. I began with study models for two design concepts, one with a circular motif and the other with a set of linear spaces. We debated the two schemes, and in the end we all agreed that the linear design worked best in the space.

There were real challenges and opportunities. The clients, who live in and own the buildings, have a wonderful sculpture collection that they display in the garden. Yet for years, the sculptures were submerged in old shrubs, and shade from the tall buildings surrounding the courtyard created difficult growing conditions.

From the start, I thought that our design

strategy should set up complexity and variation in perceiving the garden's multiple views. Some gardens are best understood from a single vantage point; others by moving through them; and still others, like MoMA, from above. Designed for varied perspectives,

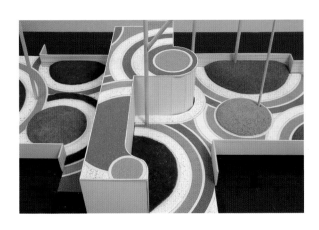

this courtyard garden may be appreciated in all three ways: from a window-lined passage and rotunda space that connects the two buildings and also from the apartments surrounding and looking down on the garden. At ground level, the linear spaces offer a heightened sense of scale, depth, and visual mystery. The walk from the north building into the passage immerses visitors in a mesh of tall aluminum-stained wood screens that seem to slide back. The linear parterres open up, encouraging viewers to pause at the curved seat in the alcove, surrounded by the garden on all sides, or continue on.

I simplified the ground plane to reveal the organic structure of the existing sycamore and locust trees. I think of them as sculptures that stand out against the grid of the buildings and their windows. We sited ornamental plantings of Japanese maple, bamboo, and magnolia for background color and texture. The older trees shelter three metal sculptures that include an Isamu Noguchi torso from the late 1940s, a midcentury bronze by Chaim Gross, and a recent large bronze, *Guardian II*, by Michele Oka Doner.

Evident in the view from the apartments above is the strong linearity of the ground plane, which leaps forth as a banded parterre of ground covers, crushed white marble, recycled black rubber shards, and blue glass marbles. These linear parterre patterns and materials continue over the passageway roof for an unbroken visual effect. On summer nights, the underlit blue marbles glow like reflecting pools under the gentle foliage of the trees.

The lighting design casts illumination from above and below to make an evening tableau rich in detail and form. In the winter, when the leaves have fallen, the ground parterre stands out even more beneath the bare trees. The view from the ground-level passage encompasses the garden with a backdrop of rising steam from the buildings' heating systems. When snow comes, the effect is soft and more structural, as the screens stand out over a white ground. Perhaps it's on these snowy days that the sense of the volume of the courtyard itself is most pure.

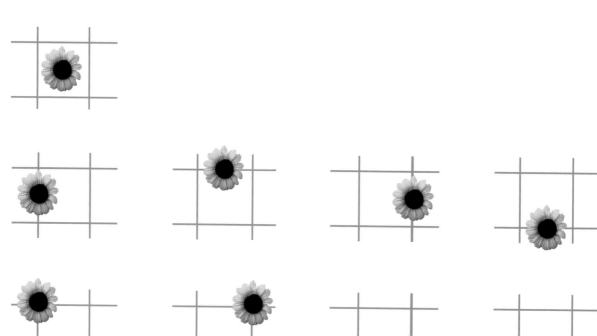

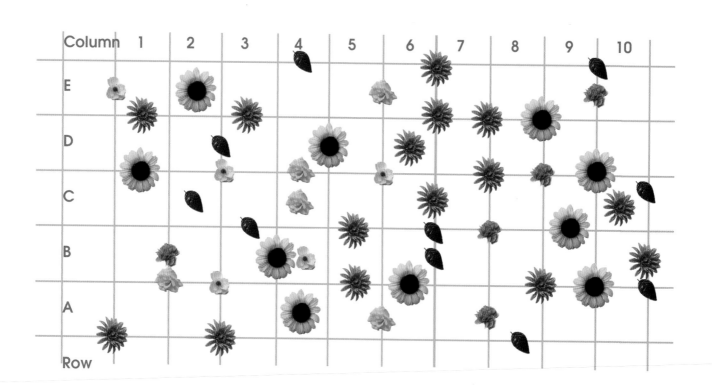

COOPER-HEWITT TRI-ENNIAL WALL-FLOWERS

New York, New York   2006–2007

WallFlowers is a series of experimental studies and installations I have been working on for several years. From early in my career I have had clients express interest in flower plantings in their landscapes. But I have never been particularly interested in flowers per se, preferring to explore the structure and form of landscape. WallFlowers is my attempt to investigate the persistent cultural interest in flowers in the context of my long-time interest in design's simulation of nature as an art form.

The WallFlowers series is based on a procedure that merges order and seeming randomness. It establishes flower patterns that are both indeterminate and organic. WallFlowers are organized on an invisible grid; the exact flower placement and choice is subject to a specified installation process. Every installation of WallFlowers is different; I have crafted them for spaces ranging from a small hotel room to a large historic mansion.

The very first WallFlowers installation, in the bathroom of my loft, used straight pins and artificial flowers left over from a party. Following this were gallery installations in New York in 1998 and 1999, Garden Daisies and Garden Deities; Hotel Eden, an installation for *Nest* magazine in 2000; Daisy Border, an installation of spinning garden daisies at the Cornerstone Festival of Gardens in Sonoma, California, in 2003; and an installation of WallFlowers in Cornerstone's garden café in 2004. I subsequently did a full gallery version, includ-

ing walls, ceiling, and floor, at Knowlton Hall at Ohio State University. There has also been a series of WallFlowers photomontages I have made from flower images cut out of garden magazines.

The most recent and most public WallFlowers iteration is the large outdoor installation draped over the front facade of the Cooper-Hewitt, National Design Museum, for the institution's 2006 Design Triennial. We hand-cut overscaled, flat flowers from varieties of bright-colored synthetic erosion-control fabrics. We used safety pins to attach hundreds of three-dimensional silk flowers to the flat cut-outs. We then chose the assembled flowers at random and placed them on a scrim in one of nine possible positions until all positions were used. Then the process was repeated until every grid space on the scrim was filled. The result was an ordered but undefined pattern.

The scrim, an expanse of fluorescent orange construction fencing, provides the overall structure. With its diamond mesh pattern, this bright, temporary material contrasted with the formality and crafted masonry of the Cooper-Hewitt building. The scrim and its WallFlowers cascaded like a colorful carpet with the openness of a garden latticework. They showed how, for just a season, the most staid Fifth Avenue mansion could become a garden in itself.

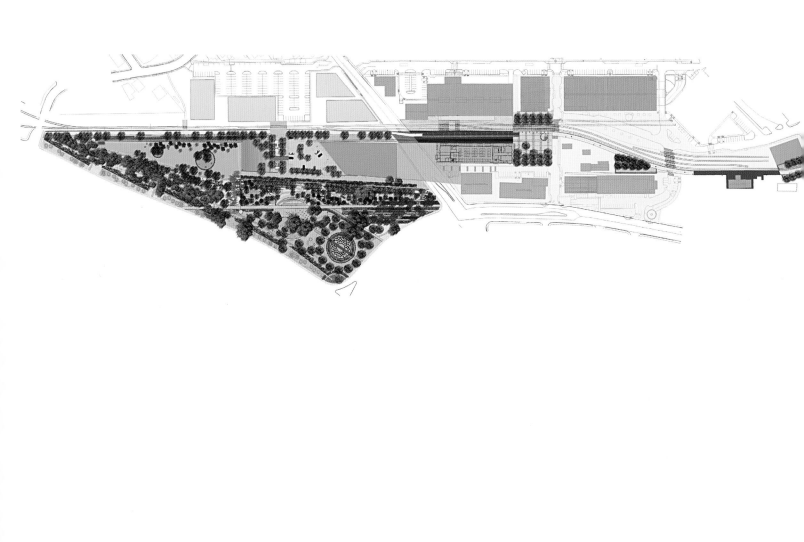

SANTA FE RAILYARD PARK

Santa Fe, New Mexico   2002–2008

Santa Fe is known for its multicultural history, which reaches back several centuries, its adobe architecture, and its historic plaza. In the nineteenth century, it was also a railroad town, a less well-known chapter that left a significant imprint on its urban fabric. The Railyard Park is part of the redevelopment of the historic train yards near the downtown core of the city. I collaborated with artist Mary Miss and architect Frederic Schwartz on the design competition. As the lead designer for the park, I also worked with the residents of Santa Fe, notably outspoken and active in community planning, to learn about the community and its social history and needs. The Trust for Public Land acted as fundraiser and park developer for the city of Santa Fe.

As the centerpiece of a newly revitalized mixed-use district, the park makes strong connections with the neighborhood and with cultural institutions including SITE Santa Fe, the

Santa Fe Farmers Market, El Museo Cultural de Santa Fe, Warehouse 21, and other city landmarks. The 13-acre space includes a plaza, an alameda, and sophisticated water-conservation features. The story it tells is one of water and of how shared stewardship of that resource builds community connections.

The park's main path follows the course where a narrow-gauge railway once ran north from Santa Fe. Our design draws on traditional northern New Mexican traditions, but the expression is contemporary. Along the paths, we designed simple benches of large wood blocks, some of which have custom-made metal backs. The most vis-ible features in the park—arroyo, series of ramada structures, children's play envi-ronment, rail gardens, and cottonwood bosque—provide community social spaces for people of different ages.

Throughout the park, water is captured

from neighboring roof areas, stored, and used as a visible element in the park landscape. A water tank in the new plaza is the central storage component for harvested water. Beneath it, a drip fountain recalls the watershed of the Santa Fe River. This water supports xeric plantings, native grasses, and garden environments. The children's play area teaches about water and agricultural history with a button-activated low-use fountain that drains into nearby plantings.

I once said to a local newspaper reporter that on the East Coast, landscape tradition begins by cutting down trees and making a clearing. The Southwest, so arid and open, is a very different setting. In New Mexico, people have historically made landscapes by first finding the water and then stewarding this precious resource. This tradition is manifest in the preserved and still active section of the 400-year-old Acequia Madre (a traditional irrigation ditch with origins in the Moorish invasion of Spain) that runs across the site. New Mexico's surviving irrigation systems are some of America's oldest designed landscapes. The fact that they have remained in operation stems directly from the tradition of the *mayordomo*, the local citizen from each generation who oversees the irrigation feature and organizes the citizens who benefit from it in maintenance efforts. This ongoing custom is one of the most unusual stories of sustainability and community effort in American culture. In the park, the Acequia Madre is interpreted with educational signs and two irrigated demonstration vegetable gardens.

of the palm desert or the natural recesses of Yosemite Valley.

The first constructed area is the Preview Park. This 28-acre space hosts concerts, dances, workshops, and other special events in order to build regional support and to give neighbors a voice in the park's design process. Anchored by an orange observation balloon that rises 500 feet for a commanding view, the Preview Park introduces prototypes of the elements that will eventually fill the entire park, including orange groves, recycled concrete works, the historic timeline, furnishings, and plantings.

ORANGE COUNTY GREAT PARK

Irvine, California   2005–2018

Known regionally as the "Great Park," this 1,347-acre project will become the heart of future districts for living, commerce, and life-long learning on the former El Toro Marine Air Station in Orange County, California. I am serving as the lead designer for a competition-winning team that includes ecologist Steven Handel, architect Enrique Norten, artist Mary Miss, landscape architect Mia Lehrer, and sustainability engineer Buro Happold.

From the start, we have sought to build a connection between sustainable design and healthful, active living. When Central Park was built at the heart of Manhattan in the mid-nineteenth century, Olmsted and Vaux's pastoral plan responded to the social and cultural conditions of the time, including the need for passive relaxation and strolling for citizens whose work involved six days a week of demanding physical labor. Today, most Americans work in sedentary jobs and, especially in places like Orange County, very rarely walk anywhere. By creating a regional attraction and a pedestrian-scale park, our goal is to immerse people in many different kinds of ecological microclimates and in cultural venues such as museums, a farmers market, and a historic timeline. We hope to create opportunities to raise questions about the relationships between global, regional, and personal health and between nature and culture.

The master plan emphasizes long-term sustainability with energy production and conservation, recycling, native and xeric plantings, neighborhood connections, community gardens, park-once-spend-the-day transit, and education programs. Orange groves will be planted on former field areas. A wildlife corridor will be established to link critical travel pathways between the Santa Ana Mountains and the Laguna coastal hills.

A formerly buried stream will be daylighted with floodplain areas reestablished. One of the Great Park's most dramatic cultural landscape remnants is the two-mile former airstrip; this will be retained along an open corridor, military memorial and pedestrian promenade. Cutting at an angle across the site, the airstrip recalls the Mall in Central Park. Also as at Central Park, we sited many of the attractions along the edges of the park to preserve the core as more quiet and passive.

One of our major design ideas, the 2.5-mile canyon, grew from an experience I had in San Diego's Balboa Park. I went there on a hot day and stumbled into a small canyon filled with palm trees and green plants. It was a separate microclimate, much cooler and quieter, and it seemed like a completely different place. The canyons of California are rooted in a mythic ideal of nature and respite, especially in places like the native palm canyons

LOLA BRYANT COM-MUNITY GARDEN

Brooklyn, New York   2005–2009

This small community garden in Bedford-Stuyvesant, Brooklyn, is a pro bono design for the New York Restoration Project. This organization has worked for years to pre-serve and manage community gardens and green spaces in underserved and economi-cally distressed neighborhoods. Working with me were structural engineer Guy Nordenson and civil engineer Langan.

Like many gardens sponsored by the Restoration Project, the space is small, an empty 40-by-90-foot lot bordered on two sides by existing houses. We carefully addressed accessibility for people of all abilities and connection to the community. The garden offers garden plots to local residents, herb gardens, fruit trees, and nut- and fruit-producing shrubs. An arbor with grapevines, columns of glue-laminated wood, and ornamental plantings are also part of the garden design.

Torqued vine panels along the sides organize the garden. These structures—another manifestation of my continuing interest in vertical gardening for tight city spaces—are fabricated with off-the-shelf fencing components and panels of expanded metal (materials also used at the Milan Condominium garden). The folding and torquing of the perimeter panels provides both screen and separation from the neighboring houses; the perspectival manipulations create a sense of greater garden depth and size. A mix of evergreen and deciduous vines will eventually cover the panels, creating a green enclosure for the garden. The ground plane is organized as a parterre of planting beds that align with the folded planes of the screens.

CONTENTS

VOLUME 6